Praise for *Circle*

"I am so excited that Monique has decided to share the *Circle of Success*! It is a great tool for anyone who is ready to grow their Young Living organization. Her passion for business intertwined with her quick wit makes this book a super fun read!"

Kelli Wright

"*Circle of Success* was invaluable for me because it broke down how to get started in easy–to–understand steps. I shared it with my new team members to help them replicate the success our team was having. It showed how we did things a little differently and made the business side of things not seem so overwhelming."

Carol Garner

"When my sister Elizabeth started her journey with the business side of Young Living, I did my best to connect her with resources that would help her business flourish. After trying multiple methods she still struggled in her approach to sharing the oils. Finally, I asked her what her learning style was. She replied, 'I love to read.' I knew exactly where to direct her; the *Circle of Success* book. The step by step format with tips helped her better see how and when to share her story. She was empowered and motivated by what she read. It was exactly what she needed to move forward."

Pam Edwards

"*Circle of Success* has truly helped me in my business because it works the way I think. I need one goal at a time...one step at a time. Some people step back, see the big picture, and run for the end game—which is awesome! But I see the end game and need to have short-term goals...aka mini steps...to get to that end game. Taking someone from one step to the next in small, reachable goals makes it easy for everyone to understand and makes the end goal much less overwhelming!"

Carmine Loper

"Awesome tool for growth! I love the way this is broken down in such a simple and approachable manner. Looking at the business aspect as a whole can possibly be overwhelming for some. Circle of Success gives us a natural step by step way to share our love for Young Living and build a healthy business. As your journey unfolds you see each step is an enjoyable success!"

Natalie Elrod

"*Circle of Success* has taken something that can be overwhelming to some people, and helped break the big picture down into achievable steps. Hard work and determination are great, but what do you actually DO? This book encourages you to move one step at a time. All the little steps end up being the big steps that are life changing. The heart behind this book is to show you how to grow and to lead others to success."

Loriahn Harden

"I am so excited to see the *Circle of Success* book available! This step by step book completely spells out how easy it is to share the Young Living lifestyle with others. Follow the steps in this book and before you know it, you will be impacting lives and earning an income along the way. As a leader, I'm constantly answering questions about getting a Young Living business started. I will be able to hand someone this book and watch them grow. Thank you, Monique and Jeremiah for making this valuable resource available for everyone!"

Tina Ciesla

"*Circle of Success* has been a fantastic framework for me to guide and coach my team. In any home based model we always hear 'make it duplicatable.' It's an effective and organic way to make Young Living's products and Young Living's business central to your conversation. This is an excellent tool to share with members and leaders to equip them in conversation with others. This is duplicatable! Thanks to the McLean's for this simple, yet educational tool!"

Leigh Ann Boone

"The simple, honest approach of *Circle of Success* helped me get started with my Young Living business. However, the real beauty is that it continues to help me today to equip other new business builders in starting their journey."

Molly Bridges

Circle
of Success

YOUR JOURNEY ONE STEP AT A TIME

MONIQUE MCLEAN

This book may be purchased in bulk for educational, business, fund-raising, or sales promotional use. For book orders visit youinfuse.com.

© 2015 McLean Essentials, LLC
Published by McLean Essentials, LLC
Salt Lake City, Utah

ISBN 978-0-692-46718-3

Cover & layout designed by Michael Durham at designerMD.net.

Printed In the United States of America.

To purchase copies of this book please visit youinfuse.com.

V2/4-2016

Contents

Acknowledgment

I would like to take a second to acknowledge these guys right here. My husband Jeremiah and my two girls Alyssa and Alayna...I am blessed because you are in my life. I love that this "YL" journey has not just been "MY" journey, but "OUR" journey. I love that we are all a team. I can't imagine doing life without you guys. Thank you for loving me for who I am, forgiving me when I mess up, and just rolling with all life has been throwing at us. I LOVE YOU BEYOND WORDS, and you know I have a LOT of words. Can't wait to walk out the rest of our journey together.

Introduction

Why hello there!

Are you ready for an AWESOME journey? Ahhhh, I hope so. I am THRILLED you decided to peek or maybe DIVE into the business end of Young Living. Besides my relationship with the Lord, saying "I do" to my husband and the birth of my girls, this has been the most rewarding and fulfilling time of my life.

Did you know that the Lord has a sense of humor? Oh He does. You see, I had ZERO desire to do the biz end of Young Living when I first got my kit. Matter of fact, when I saw it was a network marketing company, I almost didn't enroll. VERY LONG story short, I enrolled, fell in love with the product and then fell into the business side of things. I cannot even begin to describe how thrilling it's been.

I am now a HUGE fan of network marketing. I am VERY passionate about the product and the company, however I try OH SO HARD not to be a pushy salesperson. I would say my approach is somewhat relaxed when it comes to telling others about the business side of Young Living. The beautiful thing about network marketing is that YOU ARE AN INDEPENDENT DISTRIBUTOR. You can embrace your values and your vision and run with it.

I can't take full credit for this book. Jeremiah, (my CRAZY AWESOME hubby) is the one who told me that we HAD to break it down into simple steps for everyone to replicate. He told me over and over to show people how to get from one step, to the next step, to the next. I can honestly say, this concept works. My prayer is that this book inspires you, encourages you, motivates you, but most importantly...gets you moving into the CIRCLE OF SUCCESS.

Steps to the

1. **Share** – When you truly love something, you just can't remain silent. Sharing becomes natural when the product you are promoting is part of your lifestyle. This kind of sharing comes from the heart. You have something to offer to others, and they will never know they can get it from you unless you step out and share. Sharing gets the ball rolling.

2. **Try/Buy** - Once you have shared with your friends your love for Young Living, it's time for them to experience it for themselves. Some people skip over this step and go straight to purchasing a kit and becoming a member. That is FANTASTIC. Many however want to ease their way in, and we should never underestimate the importance of this step.

3. **Become a Member** – We all know it's only a matter of time before someone wants to dive in and become a member after TRYING the product. This is where the journey begins and things start to get fun. Now your friends will be able to order at the wholesale prices and get the most bang for their buck. You are going to be their best friend now that you have let them in on this secret.

4. **Fall in Love** – This step requires some patience. Allow your friends to fall in love with the products. Allow them to develop their own stories. The key to this step is to find balance. You want to check in on them and make sure they know you are there to help, but at the same time not make them feel like you are pressuring them to do repeat orders. Let them fall in love. It will happen, and happen fast.

5. **Enroll in ER** – We all knew your friends would fall in love, and now that they have, they need to know about Essential Rewards. Once you see they are wanting to do repeat orders, you need to tell them about this AMAZING program. They will be so happy to hear that they can earn FREE product. Free is a VERY GOOD thing.

6. **Join the Team** – Your friends may have jumped on the "biz" bandwagon by now, but if they haven't, it's the perfect time to introduce them to your team. Since they are ordering monthly, they can now receive a paycheck if any of their friends want to order a kit. This is where it comes full circle. You have walked them through these steps; now show them how to do the same.

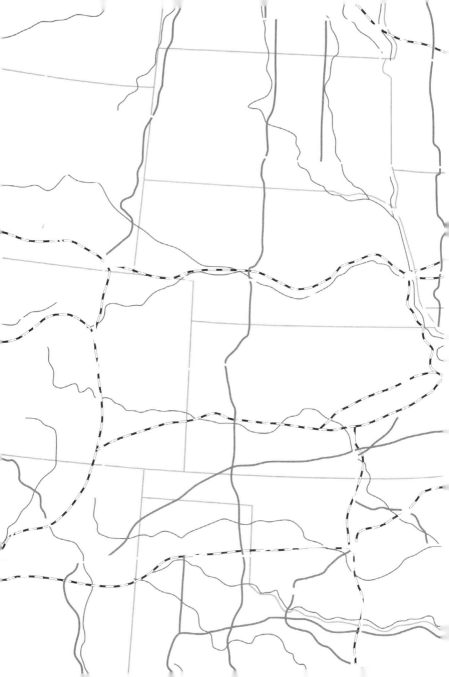

Share

The journey begins when you share with others.

The very first thing people typically say when they are thinking about pursuing a Young Living business is that they are NOT a good SALESPERSON. I reply with a big huge, YAY! Seriously, the secret to this business is sharing from the heart, NOT being a good salesperson. Sharing from the heart is easy

"When you believe in something, you aren't actually SELLING...you are SHARING."

when the products you are promoting are a part of your lifestyle. When you believe in something, you aren't actually SELLING... you are SHARING.

When you share from the heart, you are sharing passionately. Your passion sparks something in people. They want what you are passionate about. Think about this. When you tell someone of a good restaurant or movie, you don't freak out about that. Why? Because in your mind you aren't SELLING them something—you are just SHARING with them.

The Money Mind Game

Okay, I know what you are probably thinking right now. I imagine this is about the time the word money pops in your mind. I mean you TOTALLY are thinking of agreeing with me on the SHARING from the heart thing, but this is different. YOU GET PAID if people order from you based off of YOU SHARING. How can you share from the heart if you get PAID? Oh my. I get it; I promise I do.

When I first began using the oils, I would NOT shut up about it (go figure, sounds like me...right?). ANYWAY, I would go on and on and on, and then I would finish the conversation by saying I WAS NOT telling them all this just to make money. I would tell them that like TEN TIMES. Jer (Jeremiah, aka my hubby) finally told me how annoying I was being, and that I had to QUIT telling people that over and over. He actually told me it was awkward and uncomfortable, that I sounded weird, and I just needed to QUIT. I gave it some thought; he is typically right, so I decided to tone it down a bit. I was praying about it and finally was like, you know what...I know my heart is pure in this. I had NO desire to do the business end at first, but I thought, it isn't about the money; get over it Monique.

There is nothing wrong with making a paycheck. Listen, there is nothing wrong if you decided to do this TO make money. The point is, many people can't get past this first step because they let this "money" thing get in their way of sharing. You have to get past that if you want to keep moving through this journey.

Once you finally are comfortable with the thought of sharing, HOW do you share? WHEN do you share? With whom do you share? Good questions. Good questions. Let's get those answered. If these products are now part of your "lifestyle," then it flows naturally to those with whom you come in contact.

> **❝HOW do you share? WHEN do you share? Who do you share with?❞**

Embrace Social Media

Are you on social media? Share there. Social media is where I connected with about 95% of those I enrolled, and it's how I STAY connected with them. There is this misconception that when you grow your business via social media you lose connection with those you enroll, ultimately leading to your business unraveling. Well, it's a good thing social media makes it easy for you to stay connected. I believe it does the EXACT opposite of that misconception; I believe it makes for a STRONGER, more connected relationship with your team and sets the stage for a THRIVING business.

When you share on social media, you're going to reach one of two types of people. Someone you know, or someone following your journey whom you have never met. Let's talk about those people we know.

Social media turns average, ordinary people into secret agents. You know you have stalked, ummmm, I mean glanced at the Facebook pages and Instagram accounts of people you haven't seen or talked to in YEARS. You have GOT to see what that old friend is up to or who that

> **" Social media turns average ordinary people into secret agents. "**

person you had a crush on back in the day ended up with. Don't act like you haven't done that.

The point is, we do, in a way, stay connected to those we have been through the journey of life with. We ALL DO IT. When you share from your heart the love of this product, those people who follow you will see it, and it's a matter of time before they want to experience what you are experiencing. The amazing thing is, you are now connected back with that long lost friend. Now the old crush...that may be awkward.

So now that you are entertaining the idea of sharing, how do you share without sounding like a big huge infomercial? Glad you asked. The answer is balance. You will see that I like to use the word balance a LOT. Listen, I'm the first to admit I probably have lost a friend or two on Facebook because of all this crazy oil talk. That's OK. I get it—you don't want to BUG your friends. I will never forget the first month I started running my mouth like crazy about the oils on Facebook. I made a comment apologizing for talking so much about it. I had a friend reply that I should NEVER be ashamed of talking so much about these oils. My talking on and on led to her getting a kit, and she said it TOTALLY made a HUGE impact on her family's lives. From that point, it was full steam ahead. I do think my brother unfriended me, the nerve, but for every friend I may have lost by the internet wayside, I picked up a few oil lovers to replace them.

Balance Is Key

So how do you have balance? You still talk about the things you love to talk about. If you share pictures of your dog, KEEP sharing pictures of your dog. Talk about your family, your favorite movie, what you had for dinner. Come on, that dinner picture is what makes social media interesting. The point is, don't let ALL your posts be about Young Living products. When you do post about different products, BE YOU. Talk like YOU. Sound like YOU. Isn't that what we laugh about with infomercials? It's this deep voice saying, YOU CAN BUY THIS FOR $19.99, BUT WAIT, THERE'S MORE! I got the best responses from the posts I did that just mentioned me using a product and I gave no options of, HEY, YOU CAN BUY FROM ME. Give it a try; it will blow your mind.

> **When you do post about different products, BE YOU. Talk like YOU. Sound like YOU.**

I actually put the above example to the test in one of my first workshops I taught at Young Living's 2014 International Grand Convention. The class was on sharing via social media, and I had an idea. Now, I wasn't sure if this idea would work (it worked very well in my head), but the only way to find out was to give it a try.

I had a TON of different products at the front of the room. I asked everyone in the room to hold up their smart phone if they had one. The majority of the class held one up. I then asked if everyone had the capabilities of taking a picture from their phone and then posting straight to Facebook or other social media avenues. The majority did. I then asked a million people (maybe not a million) to bring their phones up to the front, grab a product, take a selfie or take a picture of the product, and just give a one liner on a social media account of why they liked this product. I told them to be honest. I told them, don't lie and say you like something if you have never tried it; be real. Say something like, "Trying this for the first time; we shall see how it goes," or "This is going down the hatch... wish me luck!" I then instructed them to say ONLY that, making sure not to follow it up with, "OH, and you can buy this from me for $19.99."

> **" This is going down the hatch... wish me luck! "**

Everyone took pictures, laughed, had fun, and then went back to their seats. I then continued the class and ended it by crossing my fingers and hoping my example worked like it did in my head. I asked everyone to pull out their phones and tell me some of the responses they got from their post. IT WAS AMAZING. In the very first class, I had a girl say she actually enrolled someone DURING the class from her post. Then person after person shared the responses they got from friends asking for more info on what they were posting about.

I am pleased to say that the second time I taught this class, it worked just as well. Oh, and later in the year, I taught this at the European Conference in London, YEP, you guessed it—worked like a charm there as well. There were two guys who got ALL kinds of comments about a post they did on Shutran, but, ummmm, we will save that for another book.

Life Doesn't Revolve Around Social Media

Now we all know there is life outside social media. Yep, there is, so let's go there, shall we? When these products become a part of your lifestyle, you USE them in public places. You are at the orthodontist. Things have been stressful, so you pull out Stress Away and roll it on. MMMMmmm, the smell catches the person's attention next to you, and they MUST know what it is. You have no issue telling them your love for it, and the next thing you know, they are getting a kit. OK, it may not always be that easy, but many times it is.

I personally don't carry my oil case with me because I want to get a new lead. I take my oil case with me because this is a lifestyle for me and I use the products daily. When you embrace this being a lifestyle, it flows into your daily life, and then it opens the door to countless opportunities to share with others, sometimes even on a glacier in Alaska.

In July of 2014, we took my parents and Jer's parents on an Alaskan cruise. We had many adventures planned for them, and the first was to canoe out to a glacier. It was going to be EPIC. We began with a boat ride to a small island, and once there, we hiked out to an area where we geared up for the canoe ride. The only restrooms available were these two outhouses, and there was a MASSIVE line for each. As my girls and I stood in line, we noticed the reactions of those exiting the outhouses weren't that pleasant. From the looks and their comments, it was going to be quite smelly. So what does any awesome, oil-loving mom do? She breaks out her lavender and puts some on everyone's wrists and by EVERYONE, I mean EVERYONE. You see, the second I put some on my wrist, and my girls' wrists, it

❝ From the looks and their comments, it was going to be quite smelly. ❞

caught the attention of everyone around. Of COURSE I couldn't allow everyone else to suffer. So I just went straight down the line explaining it was simply lavender, and that they should put it on their wrists and just smell it while they were in the outhouse.

I then went back to my place in line and minded my own business. I didn't hand out business cards, and I didn't say, "HEY, YOU CAN ENROLL WITH ME." I just gave a drop of oil and went on my merry way. A crazy thing happened once we made our way out to the glacier...a nice lady named Lisa approached me asking if I "sold" these oils. Hmmmm, why yes, yes I do. She then asked if I knew anything about the business end of Young Living. She really would like to get these oils into some yoga studios. Very long story short, Lisa ended up enrolling and is a fantastic example of how you

> **If you don't share, people have no clue they can get these amazing products from you.**

never need to feel like you have "exhausted" all your resources. When the products are part of your lifestyle, you share no matter where you are, even on glaciers in Alaska.

Keep On Keeping On

Finally, the most important thing you need to remember is to NEVER quit sharing. You may be hearing crickets after you share—that's okay; keep sharing. I've had people tell me they listened to me go on and on for over a year before they decided to give these oils a try. Don't let the crickets get in your head. If you don't share, people have no clue they can get these amazing products from you.

I went to lunch with a girl on my team one day, and she was TOTALLY bummed. She began to tell me how upset she was because one of her really close friends, practically best friend, enrolled with someone else. I found it rather odd because I knew they were good friends, and I couldn't see why she wouldn't enroll with her. I asked her how this happened, and then the whole story came out. You see, she simply was afraid to share. She had one or two people interested when she first started out. One person ordered and didn't really care for the product (crazy, I know). She allowed this to get in her head, then quit sharing.

When her best friend enrolled, she really had ZERO clue that buying from or enrolling with a particular person mattered. OF COURSE she would have enrolled with her friend had she known it would have benefited her. Lesson to be learned here...NEVER QUIT SHARING! If you are not sharing, people won't know they can get these oils from you!

Share Speed Bumps

Sharing is SO important if you want to find "success" on this journey. Many people never make it past this step because they can't drive over the speed bumps they've created in their minds about sharing. Do any of the following "speed bumps" below come to your mind when you think about "sharing" your love of oils and other Young Living products with others?

- I don't want to seem pushy.

- I don't want to bother my friends.

- I don't want to be seen as the "crazy oil lady."

- I don't want people to think it's all about the money for me.

- What if I am rejected?

- I don't know enough about all the products.

- If I share, then I have to understand the whole compensation plan. That's just too much for my brain to handle.

- I've already tried networking marketing in the past and have not been successful.

- I have friends in network marketing, and they are always trying to "sign me up."

- I've never considered myself to be good at "sales."

- I'm afraid I won't be compliant in my sharing.

These are just a few of the speed bumps I see people deal with daily. You may deal with these or some not listed here, but the point is to figure out what is holding you back.

Instead of thinking of all the "negative" ways people may view you, let's think of all the "positive" ways that you sharing can benefit others' lives. If you are reading this, it's because you are passionate about a product that has made an impact on your life and/or your family's lives. Let's go out there and share with as many people as we can, so they can experience the same things we have with these products. I believe in you. Remember. BE YOU. Share in ways that are comfortable to YOU. You've got this thing!

Oh, and about being compliant. Visit youngliving.com, they have a wealth of resources to give you that peace of mind.

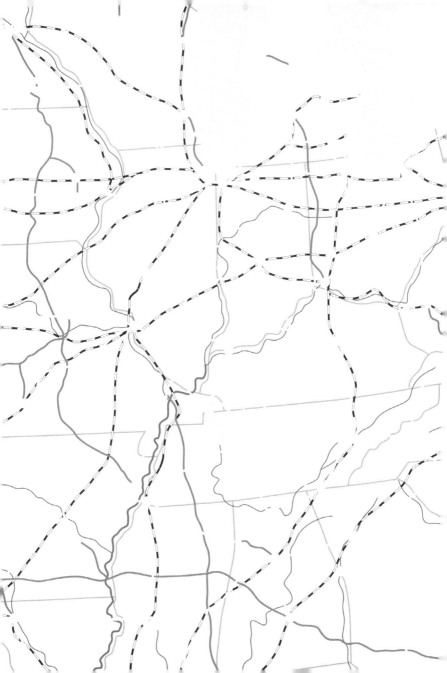

Try/Buy

A personal experience sparks your interest for more.

I don't know about you, but I was a COMPLETE skeptic when I heard about all this oil stuff. I was first introduced to them when my friend Kelli Wright and I were headed to visit a friend's farm. Kelli was having her daughter Anna Kate use lavender before we arrived at our destination. My first thought was, "Oh my word, she is just like my 'NATURAL' friend Anna Wight," (sorry Anna, I love you).

My second thought was, "Hmmmm, it smells good." Things got kicked up a notch once we arrived at the farm. One thing led to another and Kelli whipped out some lavender and waved it in my face to try.

Now, HOLD UP. I know what I'm about to say sounds dramatic—I CAN be a bit dramatic. But this is all the truth. My life flashed before my eyes. Time stood still, and I was at war with myself. I had been able to "JUST SAY NO" to almost everything remotely dangerous presented to me over the prior 36 years of my life. I mean, I signed the Nancy Reagan

> **" Time stood still for a second and I was at war with myself. "**

Just Say No campaign. I couldn't believe lavender was something I was contemplating saying YES to. I mean, did we REALLY understand how far into the deep woods of Alabama we were? I was thinking it would take an ambulance at LEAST 30 minutes to get to me, and by that time, it would be too late.

Yep, I could see everyone standing over me at the funeral, ASTONISHED at the fact that it was lavender that did me in. So, the next thing you know, I grabbed the Lavender, used it, and much to my amazement... I LIVED.

" Yep, I could see everyone standing over me at the funeral, ASTONISHED at the fact that it was lavender that did me in. "

It is one thing to HEAR about these awesome products; it's another thing to experience them. Now that you have mastered sharing and your friends are beginning to show interest, it's time to move them into the next step....TRY/BUY. Some people skip right over this and go straight to the "Become a Member" phase. That is FANTASTIC. I actually highly recommend people starting with a kit because it's the most bang for your buck. We all know though that some people have to ease their way in or that their budget just doesn't allow them to start with the kit. Even for those who say budget IS the issue, I try to encourage them to maybe save up for a month or two because the kit is just the most cost effective way to begin. If they still want to start small, you have a couple of options. You can go the sample route, or you can allow them to buy individual items from you.

The sample route is tricky. We all have tried a product and had amazing results. We also all have tried something and maybe needed to follow up with another application or just be consistent with it over a period of time. Keep that in mind when you are giving people samples. I like to give enough for them to use for a day or two. I've seen some people allow friends to borrow their whole kit of oils for a week to give them a try. I LOVE that idea. The purpose of this step of the journey is to get your friends actually experiencing the oils.

What happens when your budget doesn't allow you to just hand out samples left and right? Well, you can allow friends to buy an oil or two from you to try. Some people charge retail and some offer their discounts. I always offered my discount back in the day. Doing so actually helped me meet my monthly minimum I needed to receive my paycheck. (Have I mentioned money was VERY TIGHT for us when I began this journey?) I like this option better than the sample route because your friends get more product to use over a longer period of time.

Actually, allowing friends to order oils from me was the way I fell into the biz end of Young Living. I had recently quit work as an RN at a hospital, and our budget was TIGHT, TIGHT, TIGHT. I had ZERO interest in working this as a business, but the monthly promo caught my attention in January of 2013. My husband quickly reminded me how tight our budget was with me quitting work, so why didn't I get creative? He mentioned me posting on Facebook why I loved the oils so much and then seeing if anyone wanted to add to my order... UMMMM...GENIUS! You know the story. I got over $1000 in orders, and my mind was BLOWN at how much interest was sparked. The

> **" Actually, allowing friends to order oils from me was the way I fell into the biz end of Young Living. "**

next thing I knew, those people were having amazing results, many bought kits, and several are now some of the top leaders in my organization.

Many times just the discussion of allowing a friend to order individual oils from you will lead to a kit purchase. Once they understand the price of the oils individually, they quickly see the value of the kit and how it's a deal NOT to pass up. I have sold many kits by people simply asking to purchase an individual oil. Once your friends try or buy from you, you need to follow up with them. Ask how they liked the product, or better yet, ask if they are ready to get that kit!

One important thing you need to understand about this step is that it takes a LOT of work. You will find as your organization starts to grow, it's very hard to maintain the amount of time it takes to order oils, ship oils, hand deliver oils, etc. It's not something I continue to do, but when I first began my journey, it was the only way I could stay afloat. I have several top-ranking leaders who started out by just taking a sample or ordering individual oils from me. The hard work DID pay off!

Oh, I almost forgot to give you one final tip when dealing with people purchasing individual oils from you. You need to remember to factor in tax and shipping. If they order from you, you are going to have to cover those costs, and you need to keep in mind the cost

> ❝ It's not something I continue to do, but when I first began my journey, it was the only way I could stay afloat. ❞

involved in you getting this product to your friend. That pretty much sums up this step...Are you ready to keep moving around the circle?

Try/Buy
Ideas and Tips

- Host a party where people can come make DIY projects to take home. Think bath salts, lip balms, and sugar scrubs or blends mixed with some carrier oils. This is a fantastic way for friends to "try" the oils in a fun, relaxed environment.

- Recycle your empty 5ml bottles to give samples to those friends who would like to try an oil or two.

- When you get ready to place your next ER order, ask if anyone would like to "add on" to your order. This helps introduce them to the product and may even kick–start a conversation about why the starter kit is SUCH a great value.

- Start simple. Narrow down the list to one or two oils that you are willing to allow friends to add on to your order. One month allow people to add on lemon and orange and then the next, lavender and peppermint.

- Cute packaging with some product info is a great touch when delivering your orders. Also add how they can contact you if they would like to purchase the starter kit.

- Have an extra diffuser? Why don't you allow your friends to borrow it. They will be hooked in no time.

- Don't "break the bank." When I first started out, I couldn't afford to give stuff away. Don't feel bad if you have to charge for samples.

Finally, this step can bring up MANY heated discussions. Some LOVE this step. Some TOTALLY dislike this step and think it's a waste of time. You have to do what is best for you and what feels comfortable to YOU. What is great about this business, and really ANYTHING in life, is there is more than one way to be successful at something. When you get hung up that there is just "one" magic formula, well then you get complacent, and you stop growing.

The bottom line is, this step WILL take some work. The kit IS the best bang for your buck. However, if you need something to just get the ball rolling, to get some momentum built up, give this a try.

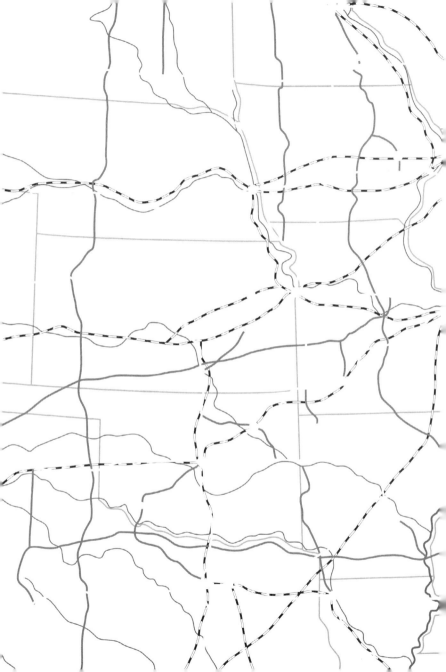

Become a Member

We all knew that after your friends experienced the Young Living products for themselves, they would TOTALLY want the kit! YAY YOU! You are about to help someone get started on this AWESOME journey. Let's talk about some concerns they may have before diving into this oil craze. Were you concerned with anything before you got started with Young Living? I know I had a few concerns.

Let's address the elephant in the room. We are all working for a "network marketing" company. SHUT UP...WHAT? I mean I TOTALLY said I would NEVER do such a thing, yet here I am, head over hills in love with what I do. You see, it wasn't "network marketing" that I had a problem

> **❝ Let's address the elephant in the room. We are all working for a 'network marketing' company. ❞**

with prior to Young Living, it was how I had been approached by others IN network marketing that left a bad taste in my mouth.

A Trip Down Memory Lane

When Jer and I were newlyweds living in Franklin, TN, we had a NOT SO PLEASANT experience with a couple involved with a network marketing business. We had been married for less than a year, both working two jobs, actually three jobs, and we had BIG DREAMS. One of Jer's jobs was working at a bank in Brentwood, TN. He had high-profile clients coming in all the time, and one day, a gentleman asked Jer if he had any dreams. He then proceeded to tell him of a business venture he was considering and that he would LOVE for Jer to be a partner. It was a new up and coming business, and he just KNEW Jer would be the perfect addition. He asked if he and his wife could have dinner with us, because he HAD to meet the wife of his new potential partner. I remember Jer coming home and telling me all about it. He was excited. He thought this was a HUGE break. I remember the night we met them. I remember cooking dinner. I even remember the meal... ummm, that could be because I could only cook one particular dish back then; HOWEVER, it was a night I would never forget.

The family came in, and like textbook, began complimenting several things in the room. They asked about a picture hanging on the wall that my grandfather painted. They asked about our dreams—if we had all the money in the world, what would we do? THEN we discovered what this new business venture was all about. If we would invest $1000, we would be on our way to success. Yep. He showed us pictures of others who invested a $1000, and now they were standing next to yachts, mansions, and fancy cars. For some reason, I just felt ICKY. I was actually crushed. Jer was too. This guy never ONCE led with how awesome the product

❝ For some reason, I just felt ICKY. ❞

was, how it worked for his family, NOTHING...only that all of our financial dreams could come true if we invested this $1000 and partnered with him. They then, after one short dinner (amazing dinner, might I add), wanted us to go to a convention with them out of state. Excuse me, WHAT? We then were on their hit list, and they called us 24/7 for the next no telling how many weeks.

Young Living Is Different

When I was introduced to Young Living oils (remember my friend Kelli, the lavender pusher?) I had ZERO clue this was a network marketing setup. I was just interested, looked it up on the world wide web, and THAT is when I saw the word NETWORK MARKETING. I actually was upset. I couldn't believe it. I continued reading on, and much to my surprise, it was only $150 to get started with the kit I wanted...NOT $1000. I also kept reading and realized that I never had to pursue the business end if I didn't want to. OH, IT WAS GAME ON. I asked my friend Kelli how to get started. She didn't know, so she had to ask her friend who enrolled her. I quickly informed Kelli that I had ZERO desire to pursue the business. She informed me that she had zero desire as well, so all was well in the world. I purchased my kit.

Many times people are fearful of ordering a kit because they think they are signing up for something that is going to obligate them to order month after month after month. While yes, Young Living does have an auto ship program, you aren't obligated to take part in it unless you want to. We will discuss that later in the book. I like to reassure my friends that they never even have to make

> **" Many times people are fearful of ordering a kit because they think they are signing up for something that is going to obligate them to order month after month after month. "**

another order. Of course, you and I both know that probably will not be the case, but I believe it takes some of the pressure off them. I always like to tell my friends that they are NOT signing their life away. I promise.

It's also good to tell them the benefits of becoming a wholesale member. Once a member, they will be able to purchase at wholesale prices whenever they would like. They don't have to purchase through you to get these discounts...they can have the product delivered straight to their door at these prices. All they have to do is purchase 50 PV in a calendar year to keep their account active.

Have you ever had someone tell you they want to enroll then never seem to get around to it? How do you deal with that? I am VERY careful in these situations. There is a fine balance of "checking" in with them and not being overly pushy. You don't want to "lose" them by not checking in, but you also don't want to "lose" them by pestering them either. There is no exact science with this, because it's going to depend a lot on the personality and the situation of the person you are dealing with at the moment. I like to check in and just tell them I'm here whenever they are ready. I tend to let them come around on their own timing.

Be A People Reader

Do you feel like you are good at "reading" people? I'm not sure I can teach this concept in a book, or maybe it needs to be a book in itself. You have to be able to "feel" people out. Read their body language. There is no magic formula. What I may do with one friend, may be completely different with how I handle another friend. When we had the scrapbook store, Jer was always laughing about how

" There is no magic formula. "

I worked with our customers. One would come in and I would greet them, walk around and help them pick out products, be all chatty with them, and they would walk out with $500 in product. Another customer would walk in and I would say hello, tell them I was there if they needed me and do nothing more than that and they would walk out with the same amount of product. It would freak Jer out every time. I could just feel that one needed more of my help and the other wanted to be left alone. Be mindful of this when dealing with your friends.

Let's Get Your Friend Enrolled.

Are you ready? In a perfect world, you are right there with your friend showing them how to enroll. This scenario is awesome because if issues arise, you can help them out. If you can't be with your friend, it's good to have detailed instructions written out that they can follow. You can email those directions and let them know they can contact you if they run into any problems. I always like to stress that they need to choose the WHOLESALE

MEMBER option. I usually go ahead and tell them the site WILL ask for their social security number but they don't need to worry

one thing about it. Let them know the reason Young Living is asking for their social security number. I like to inform them that one day a friend may want to order a kit, and Young Living may send them a check for that person enrolling.

> **" Let them know the reason Young Living is asking for their social security number. "**

Of course, THEY NEVER have to work the biz end hard, but if a friend does want to enroll, they will be compensated if they have placed a qualifying order. It's that simple.

From time to time you will have a person begin the enrollment process and then not finish it for whatever reason. To complete the order, just have the member login to Young Living using the user name and password they created and finalize the order. They go to the regular order section, choose the kit they want, and complete the transaction. You should see them pop up in your virtual office when everything processes.

Well, there you go. Your team is starting to grow. I TOTALLY knew that you were going to rock this thing!

Become a Member
Message Ideas

Below are examples of ways I've communicated with my friends during the enrollment process. Notice I try talking like myself and not too "formal." Obviously, you have to talk like YOU, but I hope the prompts below help you out.

- **Message to Person Wanting Info About the Kit:**
  OK, so I am TOTALLY pumped you are thinking of getting a starter kit. I'm going to keep it real, that's just how I roll. I was COMPLETELY freaked out when I first thought of enrolling. I thought I would be signing my life away forever. No need to worry about that, I promise. When I realized how "low pressure" this was, it was game on. You only have to maintain a 50pv order (around $50) a calendar year to keep your account active. Actually, if you don't like the product, you never have to place another order after you receive your starter kit. I have a slight feeling you will fall in love and that won't be the case. Just want you to know there is no obligation to keep ordering. I know that was a HUGE concern for me when I ordered my kit.

  Here are directions to follow for enrolling. PLEASE message me if you have any issues when walking through these steps. I don't mind helping you if you need me.

  (Insert detailed enrollment steps here. I am not going to list out in this book because we all know they may change from time to time.)

  I am just SO excited you are thinking about jumping on board. Remember, I am here to answer ANY questions you have about Young Living, the products, or the enrollment process. Don't feel like you are bothering me if you need me to walk you through things. OH, and no question is a dumb question. Trust me, I had a ton when I got started using the oils.

- **Follow Up When I Haven't Seen Enrollment Process:**
  Hey there! Just checking in with you and making sure you didn't have any issues with the whole enrollment process with the starter kit. I haven't seen it process yet on my end, so I wasn't sure if you needed my help. NO PRESSURE if you haven't gotten around to it. PROMISE. I just didn't want you to think I had forgotten about you. Let me know if you need me for anything. I'm glad to help with whatever. Hope you are having a CRAZY AWESOME day.

- **Follow-up When Someone Just Ordered a Kit:**
  YAY! I see you just got your kit ordered. I can't wait for you to get your hands on this box of goodness. I want you to know I'm here to answer all the questions you have about getting started. Remember, no question is a dumb question. Can't wait to hear back from you!

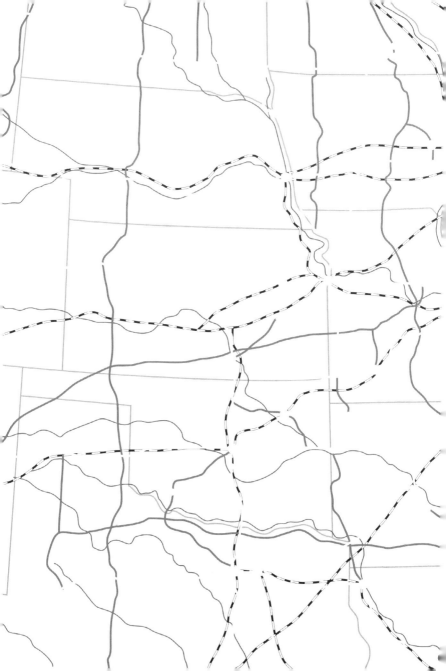

Fall in Love

Settle in, and enjoy the ride.

Your friend now has their kit, and it's only a matter of time before they are crazy, head over heels in love. You remember it like it was yesterday, don't you? You couldn't believe how amazing one little kit of oils could be. You went to bed thinking about oils, you woke up thinking about oils. Smells reminded you of oils. You started thinking of all your friends loving the oils and how they needed to be using them too.

> **❝ Well, now is the time to sit and wait for your friend to become JUST LIKE YOU. CRAZY IN LOVE! ❞**

Please tell me I'm not the only one who went into complete overboard obsession! Well, now is the time to sit and wait for your friend to become JUST LIKE YOU. CRAZY IN LOVE! However, we must have patience. I'm not sure if you are like me or not, but patience isn't my strongest trait.

Struggles of Love

Love is a wonderful state of being, however it can be ever so slightly complicated. Let's discuss the struggles of love. First, it's FINDING that right someone to love. Oh wait, we are talking about products and not people. YIKES. Well, you know what? Let's go there. Let's think of it in relation to how we view love.

We all know that you can't FORCE a person to love someone. I mean you can, but we understand how that is probably going to play out. I am trying to remember this as my girls will soon be entering the "dating" stages of life. (I think I just threw up a little, kidding, kidding). I can advise, lead, give my AMAZING motherly wisdom, but we all know if I FORCE my girls into something, they are probably going to do the exact opposite. It's human nature, or maybe I just have a streak of rebellion in me. So here is how I envision it going down in a few years.

I discover these two AWESOME guys who are just the PERFECT fit for Alyssa or Alayna. Oh, I have found the ones. Yep. No question about it. The personalities seem to fit and balance each other. They have all the qualities we would LOVE for them to have in a husband. Now, it's time to be strategic. I have to "trick" the girls into believing THEY are the ones who are discovering these guys on their own. Sneaky, it's a vital part of parenting. I can't seem too overly excited once they begin to take notice of these guys. Nope. I have to play it cool. The next thing you know, they are living happily ever after.

> **" The next thing you know, they are living happily ever after. "**

Now, of course the above statement is my attempt at being silly. I would be ever so grateful if you refrained from sending me hate mail and parenting advice. That would rock. The point being made here is that people want to come to terms and fall in love on "their" time-frame. They don't want to be "forced" or "pushed" into something. We need to remember this in regards to Young Living products.

During the "Fall in Love" stage, we need to do the following three things. We need to make sure our friends know how to use the oils and that we answer all the questions they have about their kit. We need to make sure they have all they need to get started. Finally, we need to give them some time to fall in love. We need to be helpful, but we don't want to come across as pressuring them 24/7 to make another order.

To fall in love, we have to make sure that our friend is actually

USING the oils. Many times, you will follow up with a friend, and they will make the comment that they haven't even opened the box yet. When you ask why, it's usually because they haven't got their carrier oil or capsules. This is where it's good to remind them that diffusing is an AMAZING way to use their kit of oils. Maybe share with them some of your favorite combinations for the diffuser. Giving them specific options will at least get that kit opened and help them begin utilizing the product.

If your budget allows, giving your friend a little beginner's kit of supplies will help them start off on the right foot. You can purchase a glass dropper bottle to hold a carrier oil, vegetable capsules, and Epsom salt for VERY little expense. Package these items together in a cute little bag, and your friend will be crazy excited to break it open and get started.

Finally, a great way to keep the conversation going is by sharing some of your favorite DIY projects you have made with your oils. Give them ideas of ways they can use the oils that they may not be thinking about. Maybe share a way you use the oils while cooking. Get their mind rolling with ideas of how they can incorporate these oils into their daily lives. The more they use the product, the quicker they will fall in love.

Believe it or not, there will be a time or two that a friend just does NOT fall in love. I mean, can you believe that? Well, it happens folks, and as much as we want to just shake them, it is what it is. We will still call them friend and love them anyway. We must always remember the importance of friendships, and they are NOT based on who likes using the oils and who doesn't. I try to always remind my friends of this fact. I never want this journey to create awkwardness with those I love. I am sure you feel the same way.

> **"Believe it or not, there will be a time or two that a friend just does NOT fall in love. I mean, can you believe that? "**

Friendship Is More Important Than Oils

Early on in my journey with the business end of Young Living, my dear friend Natalie Elrod jumped on the biz train. She quickly realized she had WAY too much on her plate and didn't have time to focus on the business. She loved the oils but couldn't commit to the business. She was DEVASTED to tell me and actually broke down in tears. We had to have a come to Jesus meeting. I mean, what in the world? Our friendship was NOT based on essential oils, and it broke my heart that she thought I would be upset about this fact. I reassured her we were TOTALLY fine, and that we were friends before oils and would continue to be friends even if she had no desire to do the business. Thankfully we stayed good friends. Oh, and guess what? Natalie had a change of heart. Two years later, Natalie and her husband, Andy, are leading an AMAZING team of people. Natalie is one of my best friends, and I'm sad to say that I see WAY TOO many people allow this oil business to damage their relationships. PLEASE remember that friendships are WAY more important. Okay? Okay, good. Glad we agree on that point.

Fall in Love
Ideas and Tips

Your friends can't fall in love if they aren't using the products. Here are some ideas to keep them moving in the right direction.

- Host a class specifically for those who just ordered their kits. You could call it "What's Next," or "Open That Kit," or "Kick It Up A Notch." The point of this class is to get people actually OPENING their kits. I love getting a group of newbies together and hearing their excitement for what they've been using. Their excitement is contagious and will give everyone an extra boost of momentum.

- Host a class where newbies bring their oils with them and create DIY projects. You could make bath salts, sugar scrubs, lip balms, and endless other things. Ask ways they have been using their new Young Living products. Hearing how others use items will surely motivate and inspire others.

- Host a cooking class at your home. Show new members ways they can incorporate Young Living products into their everyday lives.

- Make sure you continue to share ways you are using products. Your friends are listening and your stories still inspire them, EVEN AFTER they have purchased their kits.

- Inform your friends of the Young Living promotions that are offered monthly. This is a great way to keep them trying new items for FREE.

Enroll in ER

Earn rewards along the way.

We've all signed up for something that auto drafts out of our account monthly before, right? Have you ever signed up for something that requires money to be sucked out of your account for a year, or six months? I have, and Jer gave me the stank eye each time he saw it hit our account. It was usually because I used whatever services or product for one month and never touched it again and had to pay month

> **❝Jer gave me the stank eye each time he saw it hit our account.❞**

after month after month. THIS is what freaks people out about Essential Rewards. I like to reassure my friends that there is NOTHING to worry about with ER.

The main reason you can have a peace of mind is because you can cancel this service at ANY time. You also get one skip month in a calendar year. SCORE. Young Living is OH SO generous with how they run this program.

The next thing that freaks people out is not being sure what their bank account may look like from month to month. They don't want to commit to a certain "date" for an order to process. PERFECT. You can ALWAYS change your ER date from month to month. It's so simple. You aren't locked into one day for the life of your enrollment.

The final freak out point is that they don't want the same product month after month. They are thinking how much peppermint does one really need, right? Well, maybe that isn't a good question to ask those of us who are a tad bit obsessed with peppermint, but you get the point. The good thing with Essential Rewards is that you can change up what you order EVERY SINGLE MONTH. Shut it up right this second. That rocks, and you know it.

When you are walking your friends through these steps, you need to be proactive. What do I mean by that? Think of their "fears" and their "freak out" points. Yep. Beat them to it. Address these fears before they have a second to enter their minds. You and I both know that there is nothing to fear with Essential Rewards. We just have to help our friends feel the same way.

> **"When you are walking your friends through these steps, you need to be proactive."**

Benefits Of Essential Rewards

Joining ER is a no brainer when you realize that you can cancel at anytime, change your items ordered, AND change up your ship date each month. Yep. No brainer. HOWEVER, your friend needs to know it gets even better. Oh, it does. ER allows you to earn product credits the longer you are in the program to redeem for free product. I know, I know, this may be too much for your friend to handle. I get it. It blew my mind the first time I read this bit of information. You earn 10% of your ER's PV total in months 1-6. You earn 15% of your ER's PV total in months 7-12. Finally, you earn 20% of your ER's PV total in months 13+. I mean COME ON PEOPLE, this is crazy insane.

The benefits of ER don't stop there. Can we say REDUCED SHIPPING RATES? I mean, GET OUT OF TOWN. I apologize I'm getting a bit worked up. Clearly you and I both know all this, but can you just imagine the reaction your friends will have when they get this info?

OK, let's simmer down a bit. Let's talk some logistics of ER. You only have to spend 50 PV a month to keep your account active. Remember that you can cancel your account whenever you wish. If you DO cancel your ER, please, for the love of EVERYTHING, make sure to redeem your ER points you have earned before you cancel. Once you cancel you lose those points. This is a great thing to remember to tell your friends, nobody wants to throw away free products. I may cry just thinking about it.

When the time finally comes for your friends to enroll in ER, help them walk through the steps. Do you remember how you created steps to walk someone through the becoming a member step? Do the same for enrolling in ER. It will be simple to copy and paste in a message and send to your friends if you have these saved on your computer. Remind them to message you if they have any issues at the time of enrolling in ER. We want this to be a simple and painless process.

> ❝ When the time finally comes for your friend to enroll in ER, help them walk through the steps. ❞

Well, looks like these little baby steps are getting your friends closer and closer to the crazy awesome journey you are on. It's so exciting, isn't it? Let's move on to the final step where things get kicked up to a whole new level of awesome.

Enroll In ER
Message Ideas

- **Slightly Introducing ER**

  Why hello there. I just wanted to check in with you to see if you were crazy obsessed with the oils yet! It's OK if you don't want to admit that you are at MY CRAZY level yet. Kidding, kidding. (well kind of). ANYWAY, just heads up...if you ever get to the point of placing a second order, shoot me a message. Young Living has a program that is set up to save you money on shipping and allows you to earn back free product. I just wouldn't want you to miss out on that when you place your next order. Okay, that's all for now. Message me if you ever need anything!!!

- **Full Details of ER (after friend asks for more info)**

  Why hello there. I am SO THRILLED you love your oils. YAY! OK, so what is this "Essential Rewards" stuff all about? Here's the deal. Are you sitting down? You may get a bit weak in the knees. Essential Rewards is Young Living's auto ship program. NOW, before you freak out, let's talk. There is ZERO reason to be worried about this set up. I PROMISE. This isn't like your typical auto ship program where you are bound to something for eternity. Young Living allows you to cancel whenever you wish. You aren't locked into a particular amount of months. You only have to spend 50 PV a month to join the program. You earn cheaper shipping AND you earn back ER points that can be redeemed for free product. Months 1-6 you earn 10% of your ER's PV order back in points, months 7-12 you earn 15% back, and months 13+ you earn 20%. It's kind of crazy. You then can allow these to add up and redeem for free product.

The best thing about the program is that you can change up your ship date each month AND what you order from month to month. You aren't locked into the same date or same products. So really there is nothing to worry about with ER.

If you go to place this second order, it is TOTALLY worth giving it a try. If you think you aren't going to place any other orders, just cancel your ER. I have typed up some instructions below explaining how to get all set up. Let me know if you have any questions about the program, or if you need help getting it set up!

Again, I'm SO GLAD you love your oils. I knew you would!

If you would like to watch a video explaining ER in detail visit youinfuse.com/videos/er. Feel free to share this video with your friends.

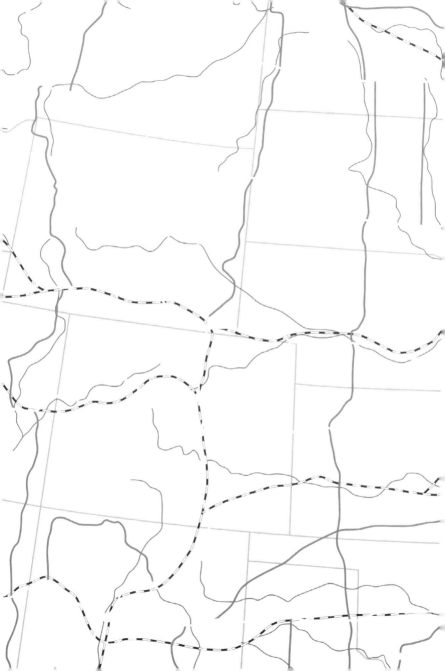

Join the Team

The journey is more fun when you bring others along for the ride.

It's time to bring this thing full circle, don't you agree? Now that your friend is IN LOVE and on ER, let's get them on the team. I like to casually mention that since they are placing these monthly orders, they can TOTALLY start making a paycheck if anyone wants to order a kit from them. You can stress over and over that there is NEVER a pressure to do the business, but usually it's just a matter of time before someone is going to come knocking their door down wanting a kit. Just let them know that you are there to help them if they have any questions. If you have a Facebook group where you train your team, offer to put them in there if they would like to take a look around to find out more info.

Let's face it—who doesn't love to be on a team? My pastor, Chris Hodges from Church of the Highlands, has done a FANTASTIC job of building a team called the Dream Team. This is what

> **❝ Let's face it— who doesn't love to be on a team? ❞**

some churches would call "volunteers," but not Pastor Chris. It's called the DREAM TEAM. This team consists of members of the church who give of their time by serving in areas that they are passionate about. Every year the church hosts a Dream Team Party. Oh, it is EPIC. It is a night you do NOT want to miss. He tells a story about the very first party the church ever hosted. It was small, just a handful of those who helped launch the church, and he took them out for a steak dinner. When word got out about this steak dinner, many other members wanted to know how they could get in on the fun. It really wasn't about the steak dinner.

Nope. They wanted to know how they could be part of the team. People want to belong. People want to be part of something fun and meaningful. You have the opportunity to create this

> **"People want to belong. People want to be part of something fun and meaningful."**

environment. I can honestly say, I am having the time of my life because I am doing life with an AMAZING group of people. We truly are better together!

You have now walked someone through the whole process of the Circle of Success. You have faced ups and downs. You know things that worked and things that didn't work. Share your experiences with your friend who is just starting out on their journey. This is where the real fun begins. Helping others be successful is so rewarding and fulfilling. When you make this journey about others, you just can't go wrong. You will grow so much quicker when you take the focus off you and put the focus on your team.

Keep walking people through this Circle of Success; teach them how to walk others through it as well. Your mind will be blown when you see how quickly your team grows. I am praying these steps help you on your journey. You've got this thing. I TOTALLY believe in you!

Join the Team
Building Community

Facebook groups are a fantastic way to build community and stay connected to those on your team from all over the world. Here are a few ideas and tips for using Facebook.

- In my opinion, Facebook "groups" have a much more community feel when it comes to staying connected than Facebook "pages" do. When creating a Facebook group, you can set it to be public or private. I LOVE this feature. Facebook pages seem harder to navigate and use for the purpose of community. You use what works best for you.

- Are you focusing on the growth of a particular leg? Fantastic. Create a Facebook group for it, and run special contests and promotions for that specific leg. This allows you to do more hands-on coaching and leading in that group to get some momentum going.

- Adam Green, the youngest Royal Crown Diamond, inspired me early on in my Young Living journey. He wrote an article on how he led his growing organization. He had one Facebook group for those doing the business and one for product users. I have to say, this is GENIUS. Having a biz group that seems kind of "secret" makes everyone wonder what is going on in there, and they TOTALLY want to be on the team too.

- I have recently started putting more focus on my personally enrolled members via Facebook groups. I created a group for those who are Executives and below—I call them Flippin' Silvers (they are wanting to "flip" to Silver). I created a group called Flippin' Diamonds for those Silver and above (they are wanting to "flip" to Diamond). These groups are working very well for this stage of our journey.

Building Community Outside Social Media

- Who doesn't love getting happy mail? I love me some social media, but it's good to go all old school from time to time. Stay connected with your team by dropping them a quick postcard or a note saying hi. I am sure it will make their day.

- Are you able to meet with your team in person? This is PRICELESS. Host a monthly meeting at your house, and ask everyone to bring some snacks to keep the cost of the meeting low. As your paycheck begins to increase and budget allows, take your teams to special dinners. They will love this time together. You will hopefully see strong cross-line friendships begin to form due to this time of them being together.

- One of the best things we have done for our team is host a "couples retreat." We took 12 couples to the mountains for a couple of days, and it was AWESOME. Many of the husbands caught the vision of what their wives had fallen in love with, and now they are working as a "team."

You know all the clichés. We are better together, and teamwork makes the dream work. It's TRUE. Everyone wants to belong. This final step is really what makes the journey so much fun. DOING LIFE WITH OTHERS. It will rock your world.

Don't Be a Stranger

Looks like our journey has finally come to an end. (Sigh.) Saying goodbye is NEVER fun, so let's stay connected. Okay? Good. I knew we were going to continue being best friends. I have to admit I'm rather chatty on Facebook, so I may drive you crazy. If you want to follow our family adventures (which are usually sure to entertain), you can search Monique McLean and hit the follow button. Are you on Instagram? We are there too. Search @moniquemclean and we will be on our way to sharing pictures 24/7.

If you are looking for more encouragement in your business or just the journey of "life," you can visit www.youinfuse.com. We have business resources as well as a blog that will keep you encouraged and inspired.

Finally, if you are on Facebook and would like to connect with a community of others who are committed to not just existing, but thriving on this journey of life...then you need to check out the You Infuse Facebook Group. This a secret group, meaning the settings are set to private, however you can request an add in by visiting www.youinfuse.com/fbgroup. Follow the steps listed on the website and you will be added in no time.

Well, time to part ways. Don't be a stranger. I want to hear all your many success stories. Now, go enjoy your journey!

GET YOUR LEARN ON WITH THESE
FUN BOOKS!

(Illustrated representation of books. Not actual size or thickness.)

GREAT FOR CLASSES!

youinfuse.com

BE INTENTIONAL WITH
YOUR TEAM!

BLING UP
YOUR TEAM'S LANYARDS
AT YOUR NEXT EVENT

youinfuse.com

BE A
COMP PLAN
GENIUS

LET'S TALK
**COMP
PLAN**

LEARN THE YOUNG LIVING COMPENSATION PLAN.

LET'S TALK TERMINOLOGY

Visit youinfuse.com/videos/comp.

Here you will find videos and graphics to help you become a master in no time!

youinfuse.com

B**OOK** STUDY

WANT TO HOST A CIRCLE OF SUCCESS BOOK STUDY?

This is THE PERFECT way to get some momentum going with your team.
WE HAVE FREE DOWNLOADABLE GRAPHICS AT SHOP.YOUINFUSE.COM.
I can't wait to see how this helps your teams!!!

Share Your Story

Teach About Oils. Sign Up New Members!

WITH FDA COMPLIANT WEBSITES

FOR YOUNG LIVING MEMBERS